General editor: Graham Hand

Brodie's Notes on H. G. Wells's
The War of the Worlds

Kevin Dowling MA
English Department, Bembridge School

Pan Books London and Sydney

The extracts from *The War of the Worlds* are reprinted by kind permission of the Literary Executors of the Estate of the late H. G. Wells

First published 1986 by Pan Books Ltd
Cavaye Place, London SW10 9PG
9 8 7 6 5 4 3 2 1
© Pan Books Ltd 1986
ISBN 0 330 50207 7
Photoset by Parker Typesetting Service, Leicester
Printed and bound in Great Britain by
Richard Clay (The Chaucer Press) Ltd, Bungay, Suffolk

This book is sold subject to the condition that it
shall not, by way of trade or otherwise, be lent, re-sold,
hired out or otherwise circulated without the publisher's prior
consent in any form of binding or cover other than that in which
it is published and without a similar condition including this
condition being imposed on the subsequent purchaser

Contents

Preface by the general editor 5

The author and his work 7

H. G. Wells and science fiction 11

Plot summary 12

Chapter summaries, critical comment, textual notes and revision questions
Book One   The Coming of the Martians 13
Book Two   The Earth under the Martians 33

H. G. Wells's art in *The War of the Worlds*

The Characters
The Narrator 45, The Brother 46, The Curate 47,
The Artilleryman 47

Setting, themes and atmosphere 49

Structure and style 53

General questions 57

Further reading 59

Page references in these Notes are to the
edition of the novel published by Pan Books Ltd,
but as references are also given to particular
chapters, the Notes may be used with any edition
of the book.

Preface

The intention throughout this study aid is to stimulate and guide, to encourage the reader's *involvement* in the text, to develop disciplined critical responses and a sure understanding of the main details in the chosen text.

Brodie's Notes provide a summary of the plot of the play or novel followed by act, scene or chapter summaries each of which will have an accompanying critical commentary designed to underline the most important literary and factual details. Textual notes will be explanatory or critical (sometimes both), defining what is difficult or obscure on the one hand, or stressing points of character, style or plot on the other. Revision questions will be set on each act or group of chapters to test the student's careful application to the text of the prescribed book.

The second section of each of these study aids will consist of a critical examination of the author's art. This will cover such major elements as characterization, style, structure, setting, theme(s) or any other aspect of the book which the editor considers needs close study. The paramount aim is to send the student back to the text. Each study aid will include a series of general questions which require a detailed knowledge of the set book; the first of these questions will have notes by the editor of what *might* be included in a written answer. A short list of books considered useful as background reading for the student will be provided at the end.

Graham Handley

The author and his work

Herbert George Wells (1866–1946) was the author of over 120 books; he wrote scientific textbooks, short stories, articles for newspapers and journals, novels and histories. There is now no complete edition of his works.

He was born in Bromley, Kent, a country town with a population then of about six thousand, only a few years after the railway came, and when coaches still stopped at the inn. His father kept an unsuccessful 'China, Glass and Staffordshire Warehouse' in the High Street where they lived, and which they had acquired through family connections. Joseph Wells supplemented the family income by cricket coaching and by selling cricketing goods. He preferred cricket to the shop and was the first player in first-class cricket to take four wickets with four consecutive balls.

Sarah Wells, Joe's wife, was forty-three when 'Little Bertie' was born. When she met her husband she was a domestic servant and he was a gardener at Up Park, a country house in classic 18th-century style. A religious woman, Sarah yearned for respectability, and disapproved of cricket. Her husband was a disappointment to her. H. G. Wells said that his father seemed to know this, and could see the point but could not see what to do about it. When he was seven, Bertie had his leg broken when he was accidentally thrown onto a tent peg at a cricket match. A month in bed recovering from his injury allowed him unlimited indulgence to read history, *Punch*, books of exploration and war, and *Pilgrim's Progress* (1678). As an adult, he expressed his gratitude for this introduction to the world of knowledge, ideas, and the imagination.

A small boy and not a very strong one, Bertie was more oppressed and frightened than uplifted by his mother's intense religion. He liked to walk about the fields of Bromley, imagining himself a great military leader, glorying in conquest, and slaughtering indiscriminately. Years later, when he was learning to ride a bicycle and writing *The War of the Worlds*, he enjoyed selecting sites for Martian depredation, feats of peculiar atrocity being reserved for South Kensington. When he was nearly eight,

Wells was sent to Mr T. Morley's Bromley Academy (30 boys, aged 7–13), a private school of rather better standing than the crowded National School. Sarah Wells felt she had to do this much for her boys, though it was a struggle to pay the school bills. When Bertie was thirteen, Joe Wells fell off a ladder and broke his thigh. Doctor's bills, and no earnings from cricket, meant that the family faced bankruptcy. When, at such a time and at the age of fifty-seven, Sarah was offered a position as housekeeper at Up Park, she accepted it.

Like his elder brother, H. G. Wells was apprenticed to a draper on a month's trial, at the end of which a £50 premium was due from his family. He worked a 70-hour week for sixpence and slept in a dormitory with other apprentices. His inattentive and casual attitude to the business led to his virtual dismissal from this first post. After a period of living at Up Park with his mother, Wells worked as a pupil-teacher for a distant relative who ran a village school, which closed when the relative's credentials were discovered to be fraudulent. He was again apprenticed on trial, this time to a chemist; but he did not know enough Latin, so was sent to Midhurst Grammar School as a boarder. The Headmaster quickly appreciated that the young Wells might earn the new government grants for the school through his scholarship in mathematics and science. However, there was no clear future in the education of a boy without family financial support, so he was finally apprenticed to a draper in Southsea. He later wrote that this was a living hell that he stuck for two years. Then he left, walking the seventeen miles to Up Park, having threatened his mother that he would kill himself unless he was released from his indentures. He became an assistant teacher at Midhurst School at the age of sixteen, at £20 a year. The only drawback was the requirement that he be confirmed in the Church of England, which the sceptical Wells resented deeply. Eventually he won a scholarship to the Normal School of Science, Kensington (now a part of London University).

After the drudgery of these early years, Wells still had to struggle on a meagre grant. He was a frail, undernourished young man, with a squeaky voice. There is a revealing photograph, taken at this time, of Wells standing formally in a shabby suit, with his arm around the shoulder of a skeleton. The skeleton is looking at the camera, as Wells looks affectionately at the bones. In the young man's free hand is a skull, also staring straight at the camera.

Wells studied science, and he was permanently influenced by the teaching of T. H. Huxley, the propagandist of Darwin's theories, who pessimistically questioned the inevitability of progress. Wells's three year course left him without a degree; he had been unable to pursue his studies evenly and had spent too much time and energy debating and editing a student periodical. Feeling himself to be a failure who had squandered his opportunity, he took a teaching post near Wrexham. A footballing accident made him an invalid for a time, and he was again sheltered at Up Park. He returned to London in 1887 when he was twenty-one, finding work as a teacher, and studying for an external degree at London University. He read widely. His BSc with first-class Honours in zoology, enabled him to work as a tutor for a correspondence college, and his first book was a textbook of biology. Another bout of illness forced him to convalesce.

Throughout his life Wells wrote comic sketches, his letters home were whimsical and witty, and his speeches in student debates had entertained and impressed audiences. He now tried more seriously to write, and his articles, scientific and speculative, were well received. He began to make a name for himself in the days when London had twenty-nine daily papers, and when there were countless weekly and monthly magazines. He found regular work as a journalist, a theatre critic in fact, for the 'Pall Mall Gazette'. This small evening paper had published his article 'The Man of the Year Million' and *The Time Machine*, which came out in instalments. Wells found himself earning a living as a man of letters, supporting his wife Isobel (a cousin whom he had married in 1891) and able now to send money to his parents.

It was *The Time Machine* (1895) that brought success and fame to Wells; *The War of the Worlds* was published in 1898. For the remainder of his long life he was a public figure with an international reputation. He joined the Fabian Society of middle-class reformers, and included among his friends the writers George Bernard Shaw, Joseph Conrad, Henry James and Arnold Bennett. As well as scientific romances, he wrote humorous novels *Love and Mr Lewisham* (1900), *Kipps* (1905), *Tono-Bungay* (1909), *The History of Mr Polly* (1910), which were partly autobiographical but also studies of social conditions at the end of the nineteenth century. Later he lived like 'minor royalty', and some of his books were made into films.

Wells was too old to fight in World War I; he wrote that he had never thought the end of civilization would really come, as it appeared to have done, though he had forecast it in *The War to End War*. In 1913, in *The World Set Free*, he had described a Utopia created after the invention of a bomb capable of mass destruction. It was two decades before scientific research caught up with the idea. Having little faith in the efficacy of politics, Wells hoped that education might save the world. He wrote social commentaries, Utopian tracts, histories, and studies of science. He had been an advocate of the League of Nations. World War II, which he described as a clash between 'dullards' and an 'infectious lunatic', made nonsense of his hopes for international harmony.

A self-educated draper's apprentice, who became one of the most widely read authors of the century, Wells saw himself too as a serious scientist; in 1943, at the age of seventy-seven, he was awarded a doctorate at London University on the basis of a published scientific paper. He was, however, never elected to the Royal Society, as he had hoped to be.

A radical, free-thinking reformer, he realized in the end that he could change nothing. He died at the age of eighty, a year after the bomb was dropped on Hiroshima.

H. G. Wells and science fiction

The origins of science fiction can be found in folklore and in classical myth and legend. The literature of mysterious creatures, strange lands and fantastic voyages has never ceased to fascinate and frighten, and the stars have always been symbolic of infinity and eternity. The epigraph of *The War of the Worlds*, taken from the writings of Kepler, the 17th-century astronomer, questions the place of Man in the scheme of things; Wells's novel is a stark answer. H. G. Wells described *The War of the Worlds* as a 'scientific romance', combining as it does the logic of science with fanciful supposition. In an industrial age, when rapid development and change are disconcertingly normal, Wells's blend of technological prophecy, fantasy, and philosophical speculation continues to be an inspiration. The most famous and telling illustration of this is the nationwide hysteria that followed the documentary-style radio adaptation of *The War of the Worlds*, broadcast in the United States in 1938. Many listeners, who did not hear the introductory announcement, were convinced that Martians had landed in New Jersey and were advancing on New York. H. G. Wells's writing had apparently evoked a helpless, uncontrollable fear of the unknown in millions of people. From Wells, the genre of science fiction inherited the inventive prediction of technological advance, acknowledgement of the brevity and the possible transience of Man's lordship of this planet, and a tendency to provide insights into the unexamined assumptions of the day.

Plot summary

The planet Mars has cooled to the point where life there is threatened. Seeking a new home for their species, Martians land on an unsuspecting Earth, near London. Puzzlement and curiosity at the arrival of the cylinders turns to fear, as the invaders first reject overtures of peace, then crush resistance. In Book One the narrator of the story gives an account of the war as he witnessed it close to the Martian landing sites; he then tells his brother's story of the evacuation of London and the battle on the East coast.

England is quickly overwhelmed, but equally rapidly the aliens are attacked and destroyed by bacteria against which they have no immunity. The narrator describes being trapped in a house destroyed by the landing of a spaceship. He is forced to observe the invaders closely, and realizes that their superior intelligence and technology will allow them to keep the human race as a captive source of 'food'. The narrator finally relates his escape from the ruined house and his walk into the empty city, where he discovers the last Martian, dead.

Chapter summaries, critical comment, textual notes and revision questions
Book One The Coming of the Martians

Chapter 1 The Eve of the War

The storyteller recalls a time before the Martian missiles fell, when our world was curiously unsuspecting of the possible existence of any older world. He refers to the cooling of the planet Mars, and describes the hours, six years earlier, when he and an astronomer friend had watched the red planet, speculating on the cause of the apparent gaseous explosions on its surface.

Commentary

The narrator, who does not give a name and whom we therefore think of as an H. G. Wells-persona, is engaged on a series of philosophical papers discussing ideas of progress. The tone of the opening sentence, with its inference of knowledge and experience yet to be revealed, challenges man's assumption that he is alone in the universe and all powerful on earth. The narrator is duly scornful, after all that has happened and is to be related, of the 'mental habits' that allow 'infinite complacency' and make men securely confident of their dominance over the material world. Ominously, he stresses the vanity of man, and points to our ruthlessness to animals and to other humans, as if to prepare the reader for an account of deserved catastrophe.

Mars, we are informed, is a planet cooling as one day ours must. With a persuasive combination of fact, logic and imaginative daring the narrator refers to the 'inhabitants' of Mars who must escape from destruction by possessing the earth. The prelude to the invasion is described so as to convey the immediacy of that time, and also to distance the reader from it and to evaluate what happened with the knowledge of hindsight. For example, the reports of the 'great light', specifically referred to as if they were historically verifiable, are made vivid by the references to the fictitious astronomer Lovelle and his description of what he saw; the H. G. Wells-narrator then comments derisively on the general unconcern, manifested in the 'note' in the *Daily Telegraph* only, at what became 'one of the gravest

14 The War of the Worlds

dangers that ever threatened the human race'.

The firing of a missile is observed by the narrator through Ogilvy's astronomer's telescope. The scene presents the narrator and Ogilvy watching and discussing, feeling thirsty, wanting to smoke. There follows a reminder of the passive vulnerability of the sleeping hundreds in the quiet towns of the Home Counties. The imminence of danger is contrasted with the utter unawareness of those threatened. The final paragraph stresses the false assumption of safety; the simple enthusiasms of 'excursionists' and the tranquillity of all that is normal appear as a challenge to the hand of fate, or the irony of evolution. Ogilvy thinks that the chance of anything on Mars being manlike is remote, but the reader by now is waiting expectantly for the inevitable.

infusoria Microscopic organisms in liquids oozing from decaying animal or vegetable matter.
nebular hypothesis Theory which suggested that a nebula (a patch of gaseous or stellar material) was the first state of the solar system. Planets were formed from the breaking away of parts of the sun.
secular cooling Slow persistent cooling.
attenuated Thin.
lemur Nocturnal mammal, like a monkey with a pointed muzzle.
bison Buffalo of the American prairie, destructively hunted in nineteenth century.
dodo Large, awkward bird, once found in Mauritius, now extinct.
Schiaparelli 19th-century astronomer, who identified markings on the surface of Mars.
opposition Earth and Mars were exactly opposite to each other, and the sunward side of the planet could be observed satisfactorily.
Lick Observatory In California.
Perrotin of Nice A French astronomer.
Nature A scientific journal in which the article referred to did appear.
Lavelle of Java A figure invented by the author; his name may be a corruption of that of another French astronomer.
spectroscope Instrument for forming and analysing the spectrum of rays.
Ogilvy Fictitious name.
tranverse Crosswise.
organic evolution Development of plants and living creatures.
bicycle An invention gaining in popularity at this time. H. G. Wells was living in Woking in 1895, and he was writing and learning to ride a bicycle.

Chapter 2 The Falling Star

The first missile falls on common land near Woking. Ogilvy, searching for the meteorite he supposed it to be, discovers 'The Thing' and watches it unscrew its top. He runs to the town to get help for the men he thinks are inside. The narrator hears of the story and starts off for the sand-pits. A journalist telegraphs the news to London.

Commentary

The missile falls on a world totally unprepared. The narrator himself may have looked up from his desk as he worked, and noticed nothing unusual in the night sky. The meteorite was seen by many, however, yet it is not until morning that Ogilvy begins his search. There follows an objective, factual account of what he sees, presented by the narrator as if Ogilvy had later told him of what had happened. The silence and the lone observer heighten the tension as the object moves. Ogilvy is a diminutive creature beside the titanic 'thing', in understanding, it is implied, as well as in size. Therefore, his concern for the 'men' inside make him an absurd figure in a Lilliputian suburbia. Henderson and Ogilvy can do nothing but shout consolation and promise as if they could be rescuers, and rap on the side of the cylinder with a stick like curious children. The town life proceeds in its homely reassuring way, and those idlers who have heard of the conveniently 'dead' men from Mars, set out to be entertained. The cylinder, however, as Ogilvy begins to realize, is there by design, though the men of this world act in their thoughtlessly busy, imitative way, like the 'eatable ants' they eventually become.

Albin . . . Denning Astronomers who are confidently referred to, as if for corroboration (see *Style*, p.54).
evidence of design Sign that the 'thing' had not fallen by accident.
potman Barman.
telegraph System of transmitting messages by electrical impulses.

Chapter 3 On Horsell Common

The narrator arrives at the pit where the missile has landed. A crowd of spectators is gathering; the narrator is invited to join the privileged group of astronomers who seem to be in charge. As the news is published in the London papers more sightseers arrive.

Commentary

The idle curiosity and mild anticipation of the motley crowd are a comic overtone to the latent menace of the scene. Boys disrespectfully fling stones, and the adults seem to the narrator to be almost disappointed at the unresponsive, inexplicable object. At a distance the storyteller himself makes little of the thing, until he can get close to it, when his scientific education alerts him to its 'extra-terrestrial' possibilities, and he is excited by the communication it might presage with another world.

Important scientists direct operations while the 'common people' impede the pursuit of knowledge. The earnestness of the self-appointed élite is as ironically treated as the popular enthusiasm for an impromptu carnival. The scene is predominantly one of holiday bustle, encouraged by the ecstatic sensationalism of the London papers, which by now have printed the news; only the reader is aware of the stirrings within the case. The end of the world may be near, but the narrator has gone home for his tea.

abstract investigations The narrator's philosophical writings.
Astronomical Exchange System of circulating astronomical information.
flys . . . basket chaise Light carts, horse-drawn.
Astronomer Royal The title of the chief astronomer at the Royal Greenwich Observatory. 'Stent' is a fictitious name.

Chapter 4 The Cylinder Unscrews

In the evening the narrator returns to Horsell Common. With the horrified crowd he watches as the first Martian appears.

Commentary

The crowd is anonymous and casually irresponsible. There are elements of comedy in the urgent and absurd exchanges, and in the excitement of the general terror and fascination. This account of the comic vulnerability of humans is the prelude to the narrator's meticulous description of his first sight of a Martian. This globular, glistening creature has intense eyes that look directly at the narrator, and a salivating mouth. The accumulation of detail creates the impression of something unspeakably vile that is also an incomprehensible threat.

The chapter begins with eager chatter and excited apprehension. The emergence of the creature brings terror and silence. The final paragraph contains images of a scattered humanity and of the devastation that is to occur.

Gorgon Creature of Greek mythology, one of three snake-haired women whose looks would turn an observer to stone.

Chapter 5 The Heat-ray

Having witnessed the first aggressive act of the invaders – the incineration of the Deputation by a beam of intense heat – the narrator flees, panic-stricken.

Commentary

The details of the now familiar common, the repeated references to Chobham and Woking, the conversation wtih a neighbour, and the narrator's acquaintance with members of the ill-fated Deputation, are all means of making the awful chaos somehow credible. Banal details of local geography introduce that monstrosity of destruction, the Heat-Ray. The white flag, supposedly a communication of the existence of intelligence, is a pathetically futile gesture, spurned by the aliens. This represents a coming annihilation of the eager enthusiasm of this world. The invaders from another world are cruelly destructive and appear to have invincible force. Wells adds to this sense of the inadequacy of what is merely human by the narrator's description of his terror, which is that of a child in the dark, fleeing from a pursuer. The story begins to take on the quality of nightmare – an hysterical flight from the invisible hand of death.

a thin red . . . circular disc A Martian observation device.
gride of wheels i.e. the wheels made a scraping, grating noise.

Chapter 6 The Heat-Ray in the Chobham Road

Speculation on the physics of the Heat-Ray is followed by a reconstructed account of the general panic on the Common.

Commentary

The title of the chapter gives the reader the essential incongruity; here is a diabolical enemy rampaging through the cosiness of the Home Counties. The careful consideration of the Heat-Ray's possible construction is rational and convincing; a closer analysis is avoided by the disclaimer that no-one has absolutely proved the details. The crowd is noisy and foolish; it is harmless and perfectly ordinary; its terror therefore the more dramatic. The slow spreading of the news, and the ineffectuality of defence preparations and arrangements for control prepare the reader for the breakdown in public order consequent upon a major catastrophe. The narrator is giving a wider impression of the chaos than his actual personal experience directly allows. He asks us to imagine, to work out for ourselves; he tells us that the news 'probably' reached nearby towns simultaneously, that there 'may have been' a crowd of two to three hundred. The narrator must be reconstructing the scene from eye-witness accounts, but the impact of the description is immediate and vivid. The reader is cleverly made to feel that he is present at events, not having them reported to him.

a chamber of practically absolute non-conductivity There is no
  normal loss of energy as the beam of heat is reflected from the
  generating chamber on to the object to be destroyed. This is not so
  much the prediction of the laser beam as the imaginative invention of
  it.
incontinently Immediately.

Chapter 7 How I Reached Home

The narrator refers to his flight from the Common, and his return to the tranquillity of Maybury. In his own home he is able to convince himelf that all may yet be well.

Commentary

This chapter is a clear illustration of how a first-person narrative allows a vivid representation of immediate reactions (for example, the derisory reception of the narrator as he speaks in broken sentences of creatures from space). It also permits a more objective analysis, which allows the storyteller to evaluate his own position at a particular point in the tale (for instance, where he compares himself to a respectable dodo). The events are seen from two points of view, that of the narrator at the time as he lived through the experience, and that of the narrator much later, when he comes to tell the whole story.

The dramatic aspects of the chapter are the narrator's subsiding terror and his relief at the comforting presence of all that is ordinary, as if this recognizable 'world' denies the existence of the nightmare. His self-protective rejection of the inevitability of disaster seems to stand for the vulnerability of the whole of a suburbia that does business at the gasworks but has no defence against a pitiless 'sword of heat'. In telling contrast, the paragraphs discussing the Martians' mechanical adaptability are calm and unemotional, clinically convincing in their relentless logic.

sensible transition He is not aware of the moment of return to his earlier state of mind.
blank incongruity The storyteller finds it difficult to reconcile the memory of the Heat-Ray with the tranquillity of Maybury.
abart . . . Thenks Common speech is often rendered phonetically; realism and humour are the intended effects.
perceptive powers in a state of erethism i.e. his excited, tense mental condition at the time made him more than usually aware of things; he remembers the scene vividly.

Chapter 8 Friday Night

The news of the cylinder and of the actions of the Martians spreads slowly, and there is little general public reaction to what has occurred. Some army units are ordered to start for the common. The Martians remain in the pit, building machines. The second cylinder arrives.

Commentary

The title of the chapter reminds us that a great deal has happened in a few hours. The story is being told with minute attention to detail. While the Martians are indefatigably hammering in the pit, having cleared the area of observers, the world of Woking and Chobham has almost lost interest in the diversion. H. G. Wells is preparing his readers for later descriptions of chaotic disintegration of social order by having the narrator comment on the curious, and possibly instinctive, refusal of the populace to react to what has happened. Their oblivion is not represented as a conscious denial of the existence of a threat; it is simply a reflection of 'civilized' life, that daily routine of the unexceptional.

The effect of the chapter is to make the reader acutely aware of the fragility of a world that imagines Woking Junction to be its unchangeable hub. The narrator refers to the stream of life continuing to flow, as it has done from time immemorial. In the same paragraph he describes the cylinder as a poison dart; and the description of Horsell Common that night with its 'charred bodies', 'burning' and 'smouldering' is an image of the hell the invasion will bring. When the narrator tells us that the authorities were alive to the seriousness of events the reader is ironically aware that their preparations for action are as ridiculous and inadequate as was the Deputation that turned into flame.

wonderful things i.e. in the sense of awe and amazement, not pleasure.
dovetailing of the commonplace habits of our social order i.e. the ordinary way of life continues, irrespective of the Martians.
ultimatum to Germany A demand that might be made to Germany, Britain's great political rival of the time, possibly resulting in war.
canard i.e. the news was thought to be false, possibly a hoax.
trenching on Smith's monopoly A London newsboy was competing with, no doubt, the famous newsagents W. H. Smith & Son, established 1792 and still a feature of today's High Streets and railway stations.
objects lying in contorted attitudes i.e. the remains of those the Martians had killed.
hussars Light cavalry.
Maxims Machine-guns.

Chapter 9 The Fighting Begins

The next day the narrator meets soldiers who are preparing to fight the Martians. The invaders reply to the attack by sweeping the countryside with the Heat-Ray. The crest of Maybury Hill is within range, and the narrator is forced to leave his home and take his wife to a place of safety.

Commentary

The first sentence tells us that Saturday was a day of suspense, a day of waiting, and much of the chapter establishes a dramatic suspense in the mind of the reader; the incongruous reassurance of the milkman, the casual speculations of the soldiers and the narrator's own feeling that the Martians are 'helpless' strengthen our conviction that apocalyptic upheaval is imminent. The controlled urgency of the narrator's departure increases the tension. No direct account of the battle is given, but the action takes place on the edge of disaster. Once more, broken intimations of destruction gather dramatic force; there is black smoke and burning; the tree-tops are blood-red. Wells's technique to make credible what is fantastic, presenting in close-up a profusion of detail. The confusion of the domestic scenes is in sharp focus, and distinctly tinged with comedy, while the confrontation with the Martians is distant.

chariot Milk cart.
Horse Guards Military headquarters.
sappers Royal Engineers.
officers were mysterious i.e. gave little indication of what was planned; perhaps they did not know?
bevy of hussars Company of cavalry.
plate Silver plate; tableware.
spanking Moving at a rapid pace.

Chapter 10 In the Storm

Having taken his wife to Leatherhead, where his cousins live, the narrator returns to Maybury. He sees the Martian Fighting-Machines, and takes refuge in his own home.

Commentary

Leaving Maybury, the narrator appears to feel that the smoke and 'quivering tumult' is safely behind the hill. His wife, indistinctly characterized, has her speech reported only, and her apprehensive reaction serves more as an aspect of the narrator's response than indicating the feelings of another individual. Despite his experiences on the common (Ch.5) the dominant element in the narrator's thoughts remains excitement, the prospect of witnessing the conclusion of the strange story. In this chapter his curiosity turns to fear.

The gathering darkness and the storm provide a melodramatic setting for his first sight, by lightning, of the Martian Fighting-Machines. The metallic monster is a grotesque parody of a human; and the narrator, hiding in a ditch, is the humbled representative of the species that only hours earlier had had the supreme self-confidence of the milkman, who had told the narrator that the Martians were to be left alone, if possible, because 'we might learn something from them'. The narrator's illusory confidence is erased by his experience of the immense power of the machine, and the strangeness of his stumbling contact with violent death in a once familiar village.

The narrator is once again a direct observer of crucial events. The effect is one of concentration, and the tension is heightened by the device of isolating the narrator in a setting in which the natural world is in a turmoil independent of the invasion, yet symbolic of its power and portent. A narrative which is related in the first person has the great advantage of being vivid and dramatic. The storyteller is the figure in the disintegrating world with whom the reader identifies, and from whose point of view he sees the progressive collapse of ordered society. The reader shares the narrator's astonishment at the gigantic construction and its mobility; his shivering wretchedness; and the directness of the discovery of the dead landlord.

cousins' man His cousins' servant.
good hap Good luck.
apparition Appearance.
brazen head i.e. the top-most section of the machine is insolent in its self-confident imitation of humanity.

Chapter 11 At the Window

From his study window the narrator looks out that night on the havoc the Martians have caused. He shelters an artilleryman, who describes the annihilation of his unit.

Commentary

From the relative safety of his home, which can only be accidental, the narrator surveys the world that the Martian machines have made desolate. Ironically, he is standing at the study window through which he was gazing on the night of the falling star. A writer on philosophical matters, the narrator is by nature and training reflective, and he considers the power of the machines. He surmises that they may well be operated by the sluggish grey mouths he saw on the common. He is prompted to consider their mysterious destructive force as an 'intelligent lower animal' might regard a weapon or machine humans had invented. He presumes that the position of humanity has altered, and its conception of itself must necessarily change.

The arrival of the artilleryman allows the reader another first-hand impression, that of the ill-fated attack on the cylinder, during which the soldier's unit was wiped out by the Heat-Ray. This account confirms the narrator's 'elusive vision' of the tripods during the storm earlier that night, invincible mechanical creatures, eerily hooded as it seems, carrying a boxed sword of heat. Most of the account is given to us in reported speech, and the individual's reactions are no different from what we would expect of the narrator; in fact, they are not individualized, and here this 'character' is a device to overcome the impossibility of having the storyteller everywhere. The artilleryman's tale reinforces the narrator's.

storms of emotion Moods of intense feeling.
trick Habit.
resinous twang i.e. this suggests the smell of burning trees and the noise of fire.
to guess, the relation . . . sluggish lumps i.e. he is realizing that the Martians might be inside the gigantic machines.
ironclad Steam warship.
unlimbered i.e. the wheels are removed and the gun is prepared for action.
in skirmishing order Spread out.

24 The War of the Worlds

scintillated Sparkled.
Titan A mythological creature of superhuman size.
ejaculatory His story was told almost incoherently in fits and starts.

Chapter 12 The Destruction of Weybridge and Shepperton

In the morning the artilleryman and the narrator leave the house, the latter intending to return to Leatherhead and then to escape from the country. Walking through Byfleet, they observe the evacuation of civilians, assisted and supervised by soldiers. Afterwards sounds of battle are heard, and the general flight becomes panic when armoured Martians are sighted. Close by the narrator a tripod is hit by a shell and its Martian killed. The narrator miraculously survives the subsequent attack on Weybridge and Shepperton.

Commentary

The narrator's plan to rejoin his wife and to leave the country is a result of his rational judgement that the struggle to defeat the invaders will be protracted, 'before' they will finally be destroyed. It is clear at this point that, despite his pessimistic appraisal of a 'disastrous struggle', he does expect the Martians to be repulsed.

The most telling illustration of destruction is the bric-a-brac of pathetic flight, littering the road beside the charred corpses of fugitives. The narrator and the artilleryman seem to be stepping through ruins, as they walk through suburban lanes deserted even by the birds. When they come upon the next line of defence and the general evacuation, the artilleryman's comments on the futility of fighting the Martians underline the absurdity and inadequacy of the human response. The narrator and the artilleryman are like veterans noting the frivolous preparations of those who grossly underestimate the enemy and the nature of the struggle.

Wells's technique of cataloguing is particularly effective here. References to precious orchids, excited children, a hurried ritual, refugees in their Sunday best, elevate the confusion to comedy. This mood is then soured by a hint of panic – the report of a savage struggle for places on a special train.

The nightmarish quality of the scene gathers force as the

narrator is caught up in the battle. The refugees are Lilliputian figures who are, for the most part, too insignificant for a Martian to choose to kill, but who may be incidentally crushed or burnt in the fiery chaos that engulfs the villages. The focus of attention is not on the people but on the colossal machines. The dominant image is of the doomed metallic giant going berserk and then collapsing into the river. At this point the description again becomes a catalogue of screaming, burning and boiling, as the narrator and the fleeing populace are helpless before the catastrophic and unpredictable violence of pitiless armed might.

shoved the chimney tops Knocked them off, but otherwise the houses were not damaged.
theodolite An instrument used in surveying.
heliograph i.e. signalling messages by reflected sunlight.
'luminium Aluminium.
sufficiently Sabbatical i.e. it was Sunday and some people were formally dressed despite the growing sense of emergency.
miscellany of conveyances An assortment of carriages.
early celebration Early Church service.
grenadiers Infantrymen.
camera . . . Heat-Ray Cover of the apparatus.
ruddy brown fluid Martian blood.
wheal Weal or ridge.

Chapter 13 How I Fell in with the Curate

The Martians retreat to the common, taking the shattered machine with them. Artillery units encircle the area in which the cylinders landed. The narrator escapes downstream in an abandoned boat. Sunburnt and exhausted, he meets a clergyman whose spirit appears to have been broken by the disaster.

Commentary

There is a slackening of suspense as the Martians retreat. The artillery has proved capable of inflicting damage and of halting, albeit temporarily, the invaders' advance. The narrator's physical condition is now poor; the events of the morning, the near-boiling water and the afternoon sun have combined to make him virtually delirious. This accounts for the mental state in which he can resent his wife's absence requiring him to struggle towards Leatherhead. In this hazy condition he first becomes aware of the character who is known as the curate. The physical description of the clergyman suggests the weakness that is his principal characteristic. There is nothing one can like or admire about this portrait – a character who is the antithesis of the spiritual strength one might expect from a clergyman. The war, to the curate, is the beginning of the end of the world, even a judgment of God. The narrator, although ill, is made of sterner stuff, and derides the organized religion that evaporates in time of trial. The reader's sympathies are with the narrator, yet curiously the curate's reaction is felt to be an understandable collapse in the face of inexplicable and unanswerable force. Paradoxically, however, the curate's despair inspires the narrator. If one Martian can be destroyed, then anything is possible, and man's duty is to survive.

a fair weakness His face was without particular form or strength.
Sodom and Gomorrah The Bible tells of God's destruction of these cities as a punishment for the wickedness of their inhabitants (*Gen.* 18:16–33, 19:1–29, and *Deut.* 23:17).

Chapter 14 In London

The scene shifts to London where the narrator's brother is a student. The gradual filtering of the news to the capital is traced from the moment when the first cylinder landed. We hear that the story of the destruction of Woking, published in the Sunday papers, had little effect, and life continued much as normal until refugees arrived from the suburbs. Rumours are confirmed by accounts in the evening papers of advancing Martians and 'Black Smoke'. Fearful for the narrator's safety, his brother is uncertain what to do. In the early hours of Monday morning all London is alerted to the imminent danger and the panic begins.

Commentary

The storyteller interrupts his narration of his own experiences in order to narrate those of his brother. This character, like the others, is indistinct (see Characters, p.46), primarily allowing a broadening of the frame of reference. Leaving the narrator in the immediate vicinity of the invading force, the author can now dramatize a wider reaction to the threat. The careful chronological progression is halted at the end of Chapter 13 and the narrator's story begins again in Chapter 15.

Elements of the narrator's accounts so far are reported in his relation of his brother's experiences. The clumsy dissemination of news, the underestimating of the causes of such disruption as the capital has suffered, the tendency to minimize the danger and then the gradual perception of it – this much is familiar, though the action is on a larger scale and the reader now notes developments with informed apprehension.

Using the accumulation of detailed observation, the author describes London just before the great panic. As the narrator tells his brother's story, he comments on it. Wells involves the reader directly with the plot, and simultaneously offers him a reflective analysis.

The final paragraphs are an inventory of communal hysteria. Six million people are possessed by one thought, self-preservation.

Martians fell The cylinders landed.
crammer's biology class The class attended by students who wanted to cover a great deal of material in a short time, to prepare themselves for examinations.
puffed Made much of little information.
cab A horse-drawn carriage, for hire.
theatre trains Special trains to carry suburban Londoners home from the theatres of the West End.
startling intelligence Sensational news.
Referee A Sunday newspaper.
church . . . Foundling Hospital As a medical student he attended church services at the hospital to which he was attached.
best clothes An allusion to the practice of ordinary people keeping 'best' clothes for Sundays.
clients Passengers.
South-Western 'lungs' Places where inner Londoners travelled for fresh air.
quasi-proclamation Semi-official announcement.
peeped i.e. the fashionable people were too well-bred to stare; at the same time they were intensely curious.
'walking out' Strolling courting couples.
tocsin Bells ringing in alarm.
sickly yellow light People were carrying candles and paraffin lamps.
ejaculating Cursing.
ten pounds Then a considerable sum of money.

Chapter 15 What Had Happened in Surrey

The Martians advance towards London. The encircling artillery open fire, and the Martians counter-attack against the hidden guns by discharging canisters that emit Black Smoke. The last act of organized opposition to the invasion is the warning to Londoners to take flight.

Commentary

Linking the time of his conversation with the curate with what had happened in London, as reported by his brother, the narrator continues the story by reporting what he later gathered from various witnesses. The narrative tone is authoritative, but because the narrator could not be supposed to have seen it all himself there are occasional disclaiming references to what 'seemed' to have happened. The Black Smoke is analysed coolly from information gathered later. The account is objective, as if the narrator were a research scientist summarizing the results of his observations. The reader's curiosity is aroused by allusions to black tubes and dark clouds rolling; 'factual' information about the substance follows. The surmises of the narrator are equally authoritative in tone. The purpose of the vapour, as distinct from that of the annihilating Heat-Ray, is the paralysis of opposition, not the extinction of society. This suggestion, and the references to the Martian need for food (p.94), prepare the reader for revelations about the Martian need to colonize.

At one point (p.93) the narrator wonders what the Martians understand of the nature of humanity. Ironically, he appears to regard the resistance to the invasion as coherent, disciplined and ultimately triumphant. This is before he understands the reason for the black clouds. The chapter closes with a sombre acknowledgement of the disintegration of government.

unseasoned Inexperienced.
ululation Continuous crying sound.
Moscow A reference to the Napoleonic army in Russia in 1812. Would Londoners burn down the city so as to deny the invader victory and force him to retreat?
discharged it gunwise Like a gun.
minute-guns Firing at set intervals, according to plan.
Kopjes Low hills.
precipitation Before it sank to earth like dust.

Chapter 16 The Exodus from London

The narrator's brother leaves London as the great panic begins. Cutting across country, he rescues two ladies from men who are trying to rob them of their pony and cart. With difficulty the brother and his companions struggle through the stream of people fleeing from the Martians whom none of them have seen. They cross the Great North Road.

Commentary

The storyteller continues the narrative of his brother's adventures. Concentrating on the complete collapse of authority in the city, the chapter is a pessimistic prediction of the breakdown of order in time of emergency. A dense mass of humanity, the anonymous constituents of any crowd who owe allegiance to no one but themselves and those closest to them, moves frantically away from the irresistible threat. The ensuing panic is as blindly destructive of individuals as are the Martians. Wells's descriptions of personal suffering are more graphic here, where the suffering is caused by self-interested fellow human beings, than when it is inflicted by the aliens. The cylinder, metaphorically, is the poison dart that brings about this 'liquefaction of the social body'. The debilitation is general. Even policemen who are called out to protect the helpless are unable to maintain any semblance of order, and vent their frustration indiscriminately.

The Great North Road is a furious stream of humanity in an agony of desperation. The general impression is of swirling dust and tumultuous roaring; the particular details are vivid: the blind crier of 'Eternity', a wagon with its wheels splashed with blood, the man with his back broken still scrabbling for coins. Behind it all is the insistent demand of the refugees – 'make way, the Martians are coming' – fuelling the terror. The accumulation of detail is by now a familiar device; the chapter is the most effective illustration so far of this means of making fantastic events credible.

There is little of comfort to the reader in this grotesque spectacle of a city in flight. The narrator does not comment on the action as he tells his brother's story; events are allowed to speak for themselves. The exodus is a mass terror that utterly disregards the existence of individuals and is sometimes self-destructive, overriding the instinct for self-preservation. The brother's virtues of courage, determination and common decency, echoed as they are in the spirit of the girl, are an important contrast to the general irrational loss of control. The narrator's brother risks his own chance of escape in order to assist apparently defenceless strangers.

The catastrophe is no respecter of age, fame, wealth or even innocence; but by the survival of the brother and his new companions, right can be seen to prevail – for the moment at least – in this part of the war within the urban world. Perhaps there is still hope, although the terror of the narration would seem to deny it. The whole struggle for life is referred to by the brother as 'hell', and the final irony is the urgent scurrying of terrified refugees towards the dangers from which the brother has emerged.

swift liquefaction of the social body i.e. a metaphor for the collapse of order.
sack Looting.
motor-cars Petrol-driven engines had been invented, but were rare and were widely regarded as dangerous toys. When the story was written the Act of Parliament requiring a warning flag or lamp to be carried by a man walking in front of a power-driven carriage had only lately been repealed.
pony-chaise Small pony-drawn cart.
no time for pugilistic chivalry i.e. the brother was obliged to kick the man while he was down.
became happy in the hedge i.e. the pony was content, feeding.
prosecuting Continuing.
Her eyes met my brother's and her hesitation ended She was momentarily nervous. The brother's very presence was reassuring.
concussion Violent shaking, shock, collision.

Chapter 17 The *Thunder Child*

The narrator's brother and the ladies make for the coast and board a paddle-steamer for Ostend. The East coast is crowded with vessels taking off fugitives. Martian Fighting Machines are sighted, moving as if to intercept the movement of shipping. The warship *Thunder Child* rams two Martians before she is destroyed. The brother's vessel sails away from an England seemingly defeated.

Commentary

The chapter offers the narrator's assessment of what has happened. The drama of the previous chapter, we are told, should be seen merely as an instance of a widespread chaos. The narrator alters the focus of the story so that once again the reader is distant and objective, looking down upon swarming black dots clogging the roads from London. Calling this 'the rout of civilization' and 'the massacre of mankind', the narrator at the same time points out that the Martians evidently aimed not at extinction but at demoralization. The notion is advanced of the invader 'hamstringing' the populace for some unspecified reason, obliquely hinted at (Ch.15, p.97). Somehow this is more sinister than attempted obliteration.

The continuing story of the narrator's brother and his companions Mrs Elphinstone and her sister-in-law, is ostensibly the important material of the chapter. However, the characters, lightly sketched when they appeared, are seen more distantly. Their escape is particularly interesting because of what they witness, the greatest challenge so far to Martian supremacy. This scene of crowded seas, ironclads in line, miscellaneous craft threading their way to safety, is visualized on a grand scale. The drama of the heroic defence of refugee shipping by the doomed warship is the central action of this final chapter of Book One. As the paddle-steamer loses sight of the remaining naval line, and the sky reflects what might be the smoke and din of battle, the future of the defence force is in little doubt. The Martians may be temporarily discomfited by the most powerful weapon mankind possesses, but the resistance is futile. Part 1 of the novel ends with the traversing of the sky by a mysterious flat, broad object. The war is over for England.

Goths and Huns Tribes who overran Europe from the second to the fifth centuries.
of the falling of the fifth cylinder See end of Book Two, Chapter 1.
chaffering Doing business.
douche Shower.
torpedo-ram Battleship designed to ram and to fire torpedoes.
leviathan Large sea beast.
smack Fishing boat.
Something rushed up . . . See note on 'flying machine' (Book Two, Chapter 7).

32 The War of the Worlds

Revision questions and exercises on Book One

Chapters 1–3

1 List information given about Mars.

2 How are the references to the Martians and their missiles made convincing?

3 List details that help create an impression of the ordinariness of life at an extraordinary time.

4 What do we know of the narrator?

Chapters 4–9

1 Describe the narrator's reactions to what has happened.

2 What are the various other reactions to the arrival of the cylinders?

3 Show how the nature of the invasion is gradually perceived.

Chapters 10–13

1 What details add to the growing note of menace and feeling of despair?

2 How does H. G. Wells create an impression of chaos?

3 What do we learn of the curate?

Chapters 14–17

1 Summarize the experiences of the narrator's brother, from the moment the Martian cylinders fall to his eventual escape overseas.

2 List details that give the impression of Londoners responding rather casually to the rumours of invasion.

3 List striking details of the panic of 'the exodus'.

4 Describe the scene on the Essex coast, witnessed by the brother.

5 What do we know of the nature, purpose and effect of the Black Smoke?

Book Two
The Earth Under the Martians

Chapter 1 Under Foot

The narrator and the curate take shelter from the Black Smoke. A Martian lays the vapour with steam, and the two leave the house. They watch a Martian Fighting Machine collecting people and holding them in a metallic basket. The fifth cylinder lands on the house into which the narrator and the curate have broken in search of food.

Commentary

The narrator returns to his own story, taking it up exactly where he had left it. This results in an abrupt change of focus, a shift from the grand scale of a battle of champions to a concentration on the minutiae of an individual's struggle for existence.

The narrator is anxious about the safety of his wife; his confinement, with the curate for company, makes matters worse, since he is denied the relief of action. When the Black Smoke ceases to be an immediate threat, the narrator's determination to find a way to his wife at Leatherhead forces him on. The sight of a Martian carefully collecting humans like so many samples or specimens is a new menace, and invites fearsome speculation, as do the red masses (Bk. Two, Ch.2, p.123) and the brown scum (Bk. One, Ch.14, p.83). The purpose of the Martian invasion, not yet apparent, is hinted at. The references to the Martian feeding requirements (p.94) and their intention to paralyse and not merely destroy (p.97) have prepared the reader for the grotesque idea of an intelligent predator, parasitic upon humans.

The narrator is now perfectly placed to observe the invader, the fifth cylinder having landed on the house near Mortlake where he and the curate are eating whatever can be found. The narrator's resilience will be tested by the danger of discovery and what must follow, and by the distraction of his morally enfeebled fellow-prisoner.

figured Vividly imagined.
circumspection i.e. careful thought is required.
contorted attitude This suggests their death agony as the poisonous vapour overwhelmed them.
Pompeii The city at the foot of Mount Vesuvius, near Naples, destroyed by volcanic eruption, AD79.
red masses ... horrible interpretation i.e. suggestion by the narrator that at the time he thought these might have been the remains of the dead.
any other purpose than destruction with defeated humanity See the veiled suggestion in brackets on p.94.
concussion See note p.30.
problematical i.e. the narrator was unclear what the noises were or what they signified.

Chapter 2 What We Saw from the Ruined House

The narrator finds that from the ruins he and the curate can observe the Martians closely. He notes that they are head-bodies four feet across, with eyes and a beak, and a single tympanic ear at the back. Their tentacle-like 'hands' are their only limbs, two bunches of eight on either side of the mouth; and the Martians are therefore inconvenienced by the heavier gravitational pull of the Earth. They wear no clothing over their grey-brown, shiny, leathery skin. They have no intestines, are nourished purely by blood, have no need of sleep, are telepathic and asexual.

The narrator also observes the operations of a Handling Machine and the growth of Red Weed.

Commentary

The chapter suspends the drama of the narrator's personal danger, and concentrates on the nature of the invading creatures. The narrative voice is informative, analytic and in part speculative, that of a scientist discussing an intriguing departure from the normal. Individuals and their emotions do not for the present concern us, and the curate is reduced to being a nudge at the narrator's elbow as the latter looks into the pit the Martians are clearing around the cylinder. Initially it is the Handling Machine that fascinates its observer because of its structural imitation of human muscles. This is a precursor of the narrator's realization that the Martians are mostly brain. Observations made at the time are amplified by suppositions and discoveries made subsequently but inserted here – for the sake of clarity, we are told. The effect H. G. Wells creates is a complete focusing of attention on the aliens, to the exclusion of the human consequences of the invasion. The story, in the sense of a narrative line, is temporarily suspended so that details can be meticulously compiled.

The Martians are 'heads, merely heads'. Injecting the blood of living creatures into their systems allows these brains to exist free from the animal inconveniences necessitated by digestion. In effect, lesser creatures are used as stomachs. The reader now recalls oblique references (Bk. One, Ch.15, p.94) to the Martian need for food. The logic of the fantasy is convincing. If these are highly developed intelligences they have evolved away from the crudity of the body, with its clumsy and disease-prone fuel chemistry and the physical and emotional complications of its reproductive system. In facetious confirmation of this, H. G. Wells has the narrator refer to a 'prophecy' published in the *Pall Mall Budget*, an article called 'The Man of the Year Million', which Wells himself had written and which the narrator summarizes (p.135). The serious point here is that the evolution of human intelligence, which the Martians may be taken to represent, might well be at the expense of the emotions that are the source of moral sympathy; reason alone, the narrator emphasizes, is 'selfish' (see 'Themes'). The narrator, a writer speculating on philosophical themes (Bk. Two, Ch.10, p.189 – not unlike a 'certain speculative writer of quasi-scientific repute' [H. G. Wells]) sees the Martians both as extra-terrestrial monsters and as extensions and distortions of human capabilities.

The chapter offers some clarification of hints made earlier on Martian inventions (Bk. One, Ch.15, p.97), their need for food (Bk. One, Ch.15. p.94) and their collecting of humans (Bk. Two, Ch.1, p.125); and it prepares for the development of the story by mentioning in understatement the Martian freedom from micro-organisms and therefore the common 'morbidities' of disease.

enormous impetus to terrestrial invention i.e. the examination of Handling Machines later stimulated experiment and invention.
integument Skin.
tympanic surface Like the skin of a drum.
pulmonary distress Pressure on lungs, difficulty in breathing.
heterogenous food i.e. our food comes from a variety of sources.

wonderful Amazing.
Tunicates Marine creatures.
a certain speculative writer of quasi-scientific repute H. G. Wells.
Pall Mall Budget The magazine in which 'The Man of the Year Million' was published, and for which H. G. Wells worked.
cardinal Absolute.
emotional substratum Ordinary feelings.
carmine Crimson.
it had no modulation i.e. the hooting had no change of key.
the suctional operation This is a reference to the sucking of blood.
some little vehemence i.e. he had written rejecting forcefully the idea of telepathy.
Lilienthal An early aviator, killed when his soaring-machine crashed.

Chapter 3 The Days of Imprisonment

Trapped in the ruined house and in constant danger of discovery, the narrator refuses to abandon hope of eventual escape, should the Martians leave the pit. The curate is uncontrollable in his despair. Martian machines can be seen making aluminium from clay. The narrator hears and sees the Martians feeding. Several nights later he hears what might be guns firing.

Commentary

The curiosity of the narrator and the curate drives them to compete for the 'horrible privilege' of watching the Martians and their machinery. The narrator is aware of the paradox that fascination and fear are finely balanced. This is so even for the curate, whose weakness of character makes matters worse as he irresponsibly refuses to conserve their limited supply of food (Bk. Two, Ch.1, p.126). We note the narrator's apologetic and ominous reference to the 'final tragedy' (Bk. Two, Ch.4, pp.148–9).

Characteristically detached in tone, the account of the machines busying themselves manufacturing aluminium emphasizes the contrast between the physically versatile appliances and the awkward lumps that direct them. The inference is that pure intelligence need not encumber itself with what is merely muscular.

The narrator courageously reasons with himself that there is a chance of escape. The Martians might leave their base or, being unsuspecting of intruders, might not guard the pit; failing this, there is the possibility of digging a way out. This rational self-control and fortitude is threatened by the debilitating presence of the hysterical clergyman, by the lack of food and rest, and most of all by the awful realization that Martians 'feed' off human blood.

The reader has been prepared for this by the narrator's allusions, made as they were with the benefit of hindsight. This is the moment in his experiences when the central character understands what the Martian invasion will mean to humanity, and what its purpose really is. Imagining that he hears voices, the narrator is startled by the spectacle of the Martian Fighting Machine, with a now visible Martian in the cowl, reaching into the metal basket for the figure of a respectable middle-aged man. The feeding takes place out of sight, but the narrator listens to the 'cheerful hooting'. This is the sound (Bk. Two, Ch.2, p.137) that is produced by the intake of air before the 'Suctional Operation'. The word 'cheerful' and the unusual absence of detail makes us imagine the worst. When the narrator actually watches the Martians feed, a boy is the victim, and the narrator's silence is sufficient description; oppressed by the horror, he loses heart, having now no real hope of the Martians' being defeated by humans. Ironically, that turns out to be true.

trick of helpless exclamation i.e. the curate's habit of crying out in despair.
efficacious Useful.
spatulate Broad, splayed.
drifting suspicion of human voices The narrator momentarily thinks he can hear people talking. He dismissed this as impossible.
vague enigma Unclear figure.
cheerful hooting This may be taken to imply that the Martians eagerly anticipate feeding.
save for one planet The narrator is thinking of Mars.

Chapter 4 The Death of the Curate

The curate is now insane, and as he is about to reveal their presence to the Martians the narrator strikes him down. The tentacle of a Handling Machine searches the ruins, dragging away the curate. The narrator narrowly avoids discovery.

38 The War of the Worlds

Commentary

The curate's madness is a bizarre parody of a martyr bearing witness to the validity of his faith (see note on the curate in 'Characters'). To the narrator the threat of discovery is palpable; the crazed clergyman intends to draw the wrath of God, i.e. the Martians, upon himself. Incongruously cut down with a meat-chopper, the senseless and possibly lifeless carcase is prey to an inquisitive Martian, and its fate must be presumed.

The remainder of the episode is one of peculiarly vivid nightmare, as a Martian tentacle examines the darkness, and the narrator is followed by this blind worm feeling for his presence.

acceptable folly i.e. what the curate had preached was approved by convention, though he felt it was empty of meaning.
bear witness i.e. the curate imagines he is going as a martyr to the stake.
one last touch of humanity The narrator manages to control his detestation of the curate, and strikes him with the butt, not the blade.
without Outside.
Briareus Creature with many hands in Greek mythology.

Chapter 5 The Stillness

After fifteen days of imprisonment the narrator is able to escape when the Martians leave the pit.

Commentary

Exhausted by privation and fear, and tormented by remorse, the narrator is slow to understand that the Martians have deserted the pit. Leaving carrion birds pecking about in the 'refuse', he climbs out of his grave-like hiding place into the untainted air of a fine summer's day; but the landscape is alien, as the Red Weed now smothers the smashed remnants of suburbia.

every scrap of food gone i.e. had been taken by the Martian, presumably to feed captive humans.

Chapter 6 The Work of Fifteen Days

During the fortnight in which the Martians occupied the pit, the Red Weed had clogged the rivers and covered low-lying land.

Searching houses for food, the narrator finds no human being nor any signs of Martians.

Commentary

The tropical growth of Red Weed in the garish wreckage of London's outer fringe exaggerates the narrator's isolation and he is obliged to seek higher ground away from the water that swells the Weeds. Starving and enfeebled, he feels that he might well be the last survivor, confronted as he is with the silence and emptiness of extinction.

One paragraph (final para. p.155) is out of sequence with the closely followed struggle. The information about Red Weed succumbing to bacteria is an introduction of material gathered later, and a prefiguring of the eventual defeat of the Martians themselves (p.179).

succumbed Died.
circuitously i.e. the dogs keep well away from the narrator, as if they are accustomed to being stalked by hungry humans.

Chapter 7 The Man on Putney Hill

The narrator meets the artilleryman again (see Bk. One, Ch.2, p.57). The soldier tells him that the Martians have gone on to overwhelm London, and he argues that resistance can only be carried on under ground. Safe for the moment, and revitalized by food and drink, the narrator is temporarily attracted by the artilleryman's vision of the future.

Commentary

Three ideas preoccupy the narrator as his mind clears. The death of the curate haunts him, although he asserts that it is a matter for regret but not repentance – he could not be held responsible for their incompatibility. Nevertheless he speaks of his time of trial, which is one of conscience. His fear of the Martians is continuous, but the war remains a mystery and a challenge. Despite narrowly escaping death in the pit, he pursues the truth of what has happened to his fellow men. Imagining the possible fate of his wife is his greatest trial. The pointlessness of going on to Leatherhead is clear to him, given the rapid Martian advance and the probable simultaneous evacuation, but his loneliness makes him seek the old world, if it still exists.

This desperate plight and sense of complete isolation teaches him humility and an imaginative sympathy for his fellow-creatures. Man's arrogantly assumed superiority has dwindled to the level of rats, dogs, frogs; and even the shadows of birds are unnerving to the hunter hunted. Philosophically accepting his condition as like that of what he had hitherto considered a lesser being, the prey of predators, the narrator resolves to live. At this point of self-realization he is ironically rewarded with humanity, the intimidating and suspicious soldier.

Most of the chapter is the artilleryman's monologue, punctuated mainly by the narrator's relatively passive reactions of the time, rather than his subsequent evaluation. The soldier's view of the war is pessimistic (see note on the artilleryman in 'Characters'), but not ostensibly defeatist. Their species will be conveniently farmed in the new world; the Martian chaos has been an efficient means of quelling opposition, and systematic satisfaction of their needs will follow. Progress and civilization, he says with a curious primitive relish, are over. With an aggressive, cultural fascism the soldier looks forward to resistance headed by those who are pure and uncorrupted by the softness of urban routine. The faithful must be self-selective and admit no faint hearts. The Martians will tame for their consumption those already half-tamed by art galleries and etiquette. The food supply, he predicts, will rationalize its predicament by indulgence in religion or pleasure, but a savage few like himself will preserve the true strain of the species, preparing for a second coming.

The artilleryman's messianic fervour rejects art in favour of utilitarian knowledge, and his mechanistic view of life is a curious parallel to Martian insensitivity; he is, like them, a head without a heart. The narrator is almost convinced by his crude eloquence. The territorial games are an extension of these fantasies, and the narrator's latent objections to the practicability of the artilleryman's schemes are dissipated by mock turtle soup, wine and cigars, echoes of a civilization the latter does not intend to revive. Logic and reason finally surface in the narrator's mind as his companion's self-deception becomes apparent. He rejects the paralysis of the dream for reality and risk.

beating Searching.
stupid receptivity i.e. things happened, but he did not react rationally to them.
fetish prayers Fearful mutterings to keep away demons, pagan prayers.
vestiges Remains.
flying machine See final paragraph of Book One, p.121.
pioneers The advance party.
the night in the observatory i.e. when the narrator and Ogilvy saw a squirt of flame on Mars (p.14).
eroticism i.e. the defeated people who are bred as fodder for Martians will pass their brief lives in decadent pleasures or, like the curate, will regard their defeat as a judgment of God.
swipes Weak beer; insignificant.
precipitately i.e. the artilleryman did not want to do anything in a hurry.
parish points Possession of a parish was equal to a point.
wasteful symbolism i.e. the narrator throws away his cigar as a sign of his rejection of the artilleryman's way of thought.

Chapter 8 Dead London

Walking from Putney Hill into the centre of London the narrator hears monotonous crying from a distant tripod. When it stops he finds that the Martians have died of disease, caused by bacteria. The war is over.

Commentary

The walk through deserted central London is mapped with street-by-street precision. A sense of the narrator's isolation is compounded by his meetings with the despairing remnants of civilization, one bestially drunk and one lately dead. The city itself is a personification of a dead world; window-eyes stare lifelessly down empty thoroughfares shrouded in black dust. The silence that follows the cessation of the Voice impels the narrator to confront, in suicidal desperation, the Tripod on Primrose Hill, and to discover the truth.

The story is being told from the point of view of the narrator's actual experience at the time, and the suspense of his ignorance and incomprehension acts upon the reader. The analysis which is added to this is made possible by an understanding acquired later and here applied with hindsight. The realization of what has happened has a profound emotional effect on the storyteller, and is the climax of his narrative, reflected in the formal style and Biblical cadences. The logic of the defeat is clear, the premise simple and credible. The Martians fade away, as diseased as the Red Weed – their vulnerability to bacteria accelerated, ironically, by their means of nourishment. The narrator stresses the irony that mankind is saved, not by its ingenuity or virtue, but by unremarkable entities in the immutable world; Nature has defeated the enemy.

sweep Chimney-sweep.
black dust Precipitation of the Black Smoke.
noise... relief The normally frightening sound of buildings on fire was oddly comforting in the resounding emptiness.
disturbed Euphemism for 'partially eaten.'
evil, ominous smell i.e. of the dead, inside.
destruction of Sennacherib A king whose army was destroyed by the Angel of Death (2 Chronicles, 32).
enhaloed i.e. carrion birds wheel around the tripod's cowled head.

Chapter 9 Wreckage

In reaction to his experiences the narrator breaks down and drifts through the next few days unaware of what is happening, being eventually sheltered by strangers. When he is sufficiently recovered he is told of the destruction of Leatherhead. He returns to his house in Maybury to be reunited with his wife whom he had presumed dead.

Commentary

The delirium and its confused aftermath dramatize the gradual return to normality. The incoming tide of life is murky and fitful; the details of the city's resurgence are a tattered slow-motion reversal of the evacuation. The personal drama of the narrator is foremost here, in a rather contrived way, as in order to find his wife miraculously alive, he makes his melancholy pilgrimage through a suburbia redeemed from the dereliction he has so recently witnessed. The setting is less sentimental here than the plot, and a sombre note is introduced as we revisit his study with its window to the stars.

A sadder, wiser man, remembering the Martians and the

artilleryman, he will in future be less glib in his philosophical speculations on the civilizing process and the moral ideas it may develop (see sections on 'Themes' and on 'Characters').

advertisement stereo Advertisements printed from plates.
'Secret of Flying' A reference to the Martian Flying Machine (p.121).
muddy ... footsteps ... stairs ... study Note the inconsistency with Ch.2 p.16.
a paper An article for a scholarly publication.

Chapter 10 The Epilogue

The story ends with a summary of how and why the war ended and what can be learned from it. The probability is that the Martians were killed by bacteria, inhabitants of a world against which they in their turn had no defences. The narrator warns that he anticipates the possibility of another invasion from Mars, and concludes that the world can never be quite so naively confident again in its optimistic belief in the promise of the future.

Commentary

This epilogue is reflective and melancholy in tone, not in the least triumphant. The self-confidence and self-approbation of the old way of life have gone, and the passing of illusions is not entirely to be regretted. The narrator, a speculative philosopher, considers what mankind may have learned. This planet may not be the uniquely secure home we have hitherto supposed it to be; and it will always be impossible to foresee the nature and timing of extra-terrestrial communication, aggressive or otherwise. The invasion has usefully deflated humanity's absurd conviction of the inevitability of progress, at the same time offering potential for enormous scientific development while promoting the concept of international exploitation of it.

The narrator returns to the idea of the cooling of our planet and asks 'Should we conquer?' The reader is denied the comfort of self-congratulation. The victory was not of our making, and there is a curious similarity between the predicament of the Martians and our own. The narrator's memories of the war override the noisy, crowded reality of his daily existence. It seems to him that the bustle of the metropolis is an unreal mockery; the underlying menace in his memory conditions his view of life. When he sees the Fighting Machine surrounded now by a tumult of children's games, he, who once thought himself possibly the last man left alive, hears again the ululating cry of the last Martian.

in conjunction i.e. apparently close, but because of the position of the sun, the firing of missiles would be impracticable.
sinuous Curved.
inanimate vastness Lifeless infinity.
sidereal space The constellations.
reprieve i.e. a delaying of the final defeat.

Revision questions and exercises on Book Two

Chapters 1–8

1 Describe the survival of the narrator and the curate up to the point of the death of the latter.

2 Into what kind of world does the narrator emerge after his two weeks in the ruined house?

3 What is the artilleryman's view of the position of humanity? What are his hopes for the future?

4 What saves the narrator from being drawn into the artilleryman's schemes?

5 What does the Red Weed add to the story?

Chapters 8–10

1 Describe London as the narrator discovers it.

2 Summarize the scientific explanation of the end of the Martian invasion.

3 Describe the narrator's return home. What are its dramatic effects?

4 In the narrator's judgement, how has the general view of the future of the world been modified by the events of the story?

5 How does the narrator convey the nature and depth of his own feelings about his experiences?

H. G. Wells's art in *The War of the Worlds*
The characters

H. G. Wells does not start with a set of characters and observe the effect of events upon them and their relationships. He paraded his lack of interest in individuality, seeing it as illusory, having a biologist's interest in the species. In *The War of the Worlds* he invents a fantastic disturbance of the prosaic lives of the urban population. As the anonymous narrator he observes the consequences himself, and is, in effect, his own principal character. The other characters are also anonymous, and for the most part indistinct. Ogilvy and Henderson are soon disposed of, and the narrator's wife is not really a character, but a crude device to engineer emotion and suspense. The brother is a projection of the narrator (who is a projection of H. G. Wells) and his creator allows the Apocalypse to be witnessed and commented on at second hand by the narrator at the same time as he suffers his personal ordeal close to the source of danger.

The curate's disintegration is in contrast to the determined courage of the narrator and his brother; and the artilleryman's reversion to a primitive type are set against the brother's common decency and the narrator's intellectual reflection. The characters personify virtues and failings that exist in differing proportions in each individual and are evident in society in general. They should be regarded as schematic, rather than as attempts at naturalistic portrayal. Their actions and feelings are credible, but the characters exist to illustrate the plot, and not primarily as subjects of interest in their own right.

The narrator

a professed and recognized writer on philosophical themes

The central character is the viewpoint from which the action is seen. He is a writer whose particular field is speculative philosophy – an interest in the possible, not the probable, and what it might mean in terms of how men conduct their lives. He describes the war, simultaneously giving a commentary on it, and an analysis of its import. Although he is a self-reliant and detached man, the events test him beyond endurance. He is elated and fascinated by the initial communication; this naturally turns to fear when he sees the Martians and what they are capable of, though he remains urgently curious. It is only when he realizes what the invasion means for humanity – a fate worse than extinction – that he weakens. His reason supports him in his ordeal by hunger and incarceration, when he is in constant danger of discovery.

The instinct for self-preservation prompts the narrator's unintentional sacrificing of the curate to the Martians, and he convinces himself that he ought not blame himself for what he sees as having been inevitable. His scientific commitment to truth strengthens his personal resolve to follow the Martians' trail of destruction, and to know the worst. He is not long detained by the seductive procrastinations of the artilleryman. Overawed by silence and the intense loneliness of feeling that he is the last man left alive, he is on the edge of despair. The release from his personal agony, together with a returning sense of a future for mankind, undermines his grasp on reality. His breakdown is simply a necessary reconstitution of his overtaxed strength, physical and mental. Although the narrator is the human centre of interest in everything that happens in the story, he is nevertheless more interesting and important as analyst and speculator. At the beginning of the novel he is writing a paper, and occasionally he looks out at the stars. The paper is a speculation on what might happen in centuries to come, and the narrator's adventures dramatize his theorizing.

The brother

in London when the Martians fell at Woking

The narrator's younger brother is introduced in Chapter 14. A medical student in London, he leaves the city in the great panic and eventually escapes overseas, witnessing the attack made by the *Thunder Child* on the tripods. In Book Two he does not appear. He is an anonymous extension of the narrator, and personifies unassuming conventional decency. His rescue and subsequent guardianship of Mrs Elphinstone and her sister-in-law is selfless and unflinching. The brother's strength of character, and his solid, undemonstrative virtues, like those of the narrator, are in striking contrast to the brutish terror of the fleeing masses and the chilling insensitivity of the Martians.

The curate

the tremendous tragedy in which he had been involved . . . had driven him to the very edge of his reason

The curate's terror is understandable and, in a way, a normal reaction to the inconceivable alien menace. His self-pitying cowardice makes him an impossibly unsympathetic character. It is difficult not to anticipate eagerly his finally being dragged away by an inquisitive tentacle. The failure of this representative of organized religion to withstand disaster still leaves the narrator able to pray, and eventually to thank God for his deliverance. In his madness the curate expresses his guilt and inadequacy; he has sold his spiritual office for material gain, and by teaching the poor to acquiesce, to accept their miserable lot gratefully, he feels he has betrayed his calling. For him the Martians are an avenging God, demanding sacrifice. We must remember that the world in which the curate has lived can never again exist; there is no provision in scripture or theology for the existence of intelligent, sentient, extra-terrestrial beings. The narrator is less vulnerable; by profession he is a practical man, acting on observation and experiment, and so finds it possible to adapt to the absence of certainty.

The artilleryman

strange undisciplined dreamer of great things

At first the soldier is indistinctly characterized; he is simply a companion observer with the narrator as they witness the gradual disintegration of a society overwhelmed by a force that it cannot withstand (see commentaries on Bk. One, Chs.11,12). The artilleryman sees that all is lost. Separated in the destruction of Weybridge and Shepperton, the artilleryman and the narrator meet again on Putney Hill sixteen days later. Now the soldier is a wild dreamer who sees himself founder of a subterranean master race, a future champion of mankind, defeating the Martians by capturing one of their Fighting Machines (see commentary on Bk. Two, Ch.7). He offers the narrator champagne and cigars, as they play card games for territory in what will be a new world. When the narrator meets him he is dirty and dishevelled, piratically defending his patch, i.e. his food supply, against predators. Recognizing the narrator, he repeats that it is all up with humanity, and forecasts a Martian cultivation of tame human fodder. As he elaborates his vision, it becomes apparent that he relishes the demise of a civilization that he seems to regard as decadent. The artilleryman scorns those who will accommodate themselves to Martian rule, and talks of purifying the race. Able-bodied, clean-minded men will reject the weak sentimentalists, who ought to die, so that they do not taint the race. Life will be real again. The master race will, paradoxically, live in the drains meanwhile, preparing for the day of resurrection. The artilleryman's ramblings carry a hypnotic conviction. The narrator is mesmerized, until he realizes that the fanatic has spent a week digging a miserable hole, designed theoretically to reach the main drain on Putney Hill. The man is a pitiful fantasist, scheming madly, as impotent as the rest of humanity. His brutish determination is unedifying; his hatred of his fellows, his urge to command and to destroy, make him a regrettable survivor of a race implicitly condemned by his own character.

Setting, themes and atmosphere

Setting

The setting of *The War of the Worlds* is the South-East of England in late Victorian times, the action of the story supposedly taking place well into the twentieth-century. The topographical detail is exact, and the reader would find a contemporary map of London and Surrey an interesting and useful source of reference. The population of London was rapidly increasing, and villages like Maybury, where Wells lived for a time, were about to be swallowed by urban sprawl. The *world* of the story is that of the 1890s, when Wells was writing the book: the days of steamships, telegraph, cheap newspapers and magazines, railways, bicycles, gas-lighting and music-halls, but not yet cars, aeroplanes, telephones or radio.

The acceleration of scientific advance was beginning to be the feature of life that we know. The end of a century, like the end of any cycle of time, is naturally a period for reflection and anticipation. What might the future hold for man, the ingenious parasite, the inventive destroyer? Wells's interest in biology and astronomy reflects an important aspect of the intellectual climate of the time. Charles Darwin's *Origin of the Species* (1859), published before Wells was born, argued the idea of natural selection and the survival of the fittest; that Man was not made in the image and likeness of the Creator, but had evolved from something close to an ape, and that unchallenged dominance of an inherently hostile environment might not be assumed. Astronomers such as Schiaparelli and Lowell, who are referred to in the text, considered that the markings, or 'canals', visible on Mars might be artificial, and therefore be evidence of Life. Wells was interested in the idea that there might be Life on Mars, and in how it might differ from Life in Woking. To bring these worlds into dramatic confrontation Wells used a realistic, entirely credible, contemporary suburbia as the setting for his scientific fairy-tale of gigantic monsters from Space.

Themes

The War of the Worlds is a chronicle of doom, and its principal themes are interrelated:

1 complacent assumptions of evolution and progress are fatuous;

2 Science which enlightens may also bring disaster;

3 the Future as a great hope and a deep fear;

4 the possibility of invasion and colonization by a more powerful and equally ruthless species;

5 the possibility of encounters with extra-terrestrial forces;

6 warfare as cataclysm;

7 civilization is a frail organism.

The idea for the novel came from a chance remark of Wells's brother Frank: 'Suppose some beings from another planet were to drop out of the sky suddenly and begin laying about them here.' Wells describes the apocalyptic overthrow of man just at the point of his greatest expansion of knowledge. Observing that, for every civilization 'the hour of its complete ascendancy has been the eve of its entire overthrow', there is a gloomy relish in the descriptions of the destruction of suburban London by intelligent aliens in insuperable machines. An ironically neat conclusion to an unheroic world history would be the colonization of the Earth and its peoples by disembodied brains from outer space. The dominant species would suffer the fate it self-righteously metes out to the weaker; the predator would suffer the universal nightmare of becoming prey.

Man is presented for the most part unsympathetically as a feeble and degenerate species, earnestly assuring itself of its own significance by the acquisition and enjoyment of the vulgar wonders of the day. Newspapers and excursions are no safeguard against the moral paralysis of panic. The exodus from London is cruelly frantic, greed being the only failing that competes with fear. The brutish indulgence of pleasure of the urban proletariat invites exploitation by newspaper sellers and keepers of public houses as the city's mask of sophistication fades. From its opening sentences the novel stresses the pretentious fragility of human thought and behaviour, and points to the collapse of a civilization founded on expediency and self-interest.

Wells's scientific romances are speculations on Time, Change and the Future. He was fascinated by the transient fragility of the ordinary community and awed by the infinity of Time. Science was an essential part of his Utopian hope for a brighter future, yet he was aware of 'the dangers of power without control, the development of the intelligence at the expense of human sympathy'. The worlds at war are in truth those of the present and the future. The Martians are Man in the Year Million.

Wells's view of evolutionary progress was qualified by the second law of thermodynamics: the inevitable cooling of the sun, and therefore the earth, must ultimately put an end to the most optimistic hopes. The argument of the scientific romances is that the only certainty is millenial darkness, and though H. G. Wells was clearly an enthusiast for education, science and technology, a technophile who enjoyed conjecture, it is Nature that has the last word in the story and will finally determine the future.

The War of the Worlds forecasts space-flight, laser-beams, poison gas, and all the mass destruction of modern warfare, yet H. G. Wells declared that his stories, unlike those of Jules Verne, did not deal with possible things; he said that they were exercises of the imagination in quite a different field. He set out to write fantasies which were also parables; the imaginative creation of the paraphernalia of technocracy was important only for what it could reveal about the human condition.

In *The War of the Worlds* the annihilation of claustrophobic normality appears to be a Judgment, or perhaps the anarchic swipe of the eternal megalomaniac artilleryman. Neither the narrator nor the unlovable figures he observes are responsible for what happens; they are there to suffer and he is there to speculate on what it all means – an awful warning. H. G. Wells has often been referred to as the time traveller, the man who invented tomorrow; and he implies in *The War of the Worlds* that, although the odds are against survival, the battle is worth fighting. In writing his own epitaph he expressed his exasperation: 'I told you so, you *damned* fools.' The italics are his.

Atmosphere

The story is an account of a war, and it begins by establishing a 'phoney war' atmosphere with a populace casually inquisitive at the arrival of the cylinders, a tardy and inept military response, and the general suburban insensitivity of impending doom. Possessing weapons against which there is no defence and showing no respect whatever for life, the aggressors quickly bring chaos and inspire panic. The descriptions of the random destruction of battle and the flight of refugees are convincing, and a fatalistic prediction of the history of the twentieth century.

The atmosphere is tormented and hellish, with mankind squirming in the grasp of the Beast. The nature of that fearsome figure of the imagination dominates the book: child-like humanity is pursued by a slow-moving reptilian vampire. The monsters' technological brilliance, and the total absence of the intention to communicate with their prey, produce a feeling of helpless terror. Total war is not seen as a phenomenon one can endure. Imagery of hellfire and damnation dramatizes the death of a city. Disease shrivels the troll-like strength of the invader, and at the end of the story it is not the jubilant atmosphere of redemption that is compelling, but the narrator's memory of silence and loneliness.

Structure and style

Structure

Given the realistic contemporary setting, and the hypothesis of the disruption of the natural order, the novel is a logical projection of what might happen. Its structure is relentlessly chronological. Chapter headings log events, and the narrator constantly refers to time, measuring out the two-and-a-half weeks of the war, and recording the arrival of the cylinders. The narrator is made the primary observer, and what he does not witness directly is absorbed from eye-witnesses and reported later with the identical dramatic immediacy given to the narrator's account of his personal experiences. In the case of the brother's adventures, the other observer is present at events which the narrator could not have seen or experienced; the brother's story is inserted into the main narrative, and the narrator retells it as if it were his own. This arrangement retains the vivid directness of a first person narrative, and attempts to avoid its limitations; the narrator watches the world of the Martians, while his brother watches the collapse of our world. The narrator is also in fact writing the history of the war, occasionally referring to other 'sources' for elaboration or confirmation, giving objective scientific analysis, and evaluating events from a distance, with the advantage of hindsight.

The narrator observes, experiences, reacts and reflects. Oddly privileged by his incarceration in uniquely close proximity to the aliens, after his ordeal by fear and starvation, he begins to understand the human condition – the struggle for survival.

Style

The narrator (the literary persona assumed by the author) relates events both ordinary and incredible in a restrained, detached tone. The commentary continuously provides details of location and of historical setting, so making the fantastic seem real. Observations made at the time are supported by cross references to scientists and their theories, journals, and later discoveries made subsequently, thus giving to the style a documentary authenticity. This objective, realistic aspect of Wells's style is sometimes relaxed, when, for example, the narrator gently derides the vulnerability of busy and respectable pleasure seekers (p.36; p.65). In the particularly dramatic episodes the style retains its formality, and through imagery and rhythm expands to a sweeping grandeur reminiscent of myth (p.98 and Bk. Two, Ch.8).

The narrator is presenting a history of the war for the edification of future generations. The book opens with the words, 'No one would have believed . . .'; the narrator's task is to enlighten and even 'remind the reader' of the vanity and blindness of Man. The objective style in which this is done is calm yet commanding, persuading the reader to accept the narrator's point of view. 'We' come to understand the implication of the war just as the narrator does as he lives through it; the phrase 'I remember' gives recurrent emphasis to the personal nature of the account, which is at the same time a record.

The intelligent and sensitive narrative voice documents the course of the war, the progress of the Heat-Ray down the Chobham Road (Bk. One, Ch.6). The references are initially to actual scientific investigations (pp.10–11) and historical figures (e.g. Schiaparelli), and later to fictitious research (e.g. Carver, pp.189–90). The latter 'evidence', although false, contributes, however, to the realism of the style, as does, for example, the 'admission' that 'we are still ignorant of the nature' of the Black Smoke. The style is predominantly literal, as befits a scientist and philosopher: recording, observing, categorizing and inferring (see also Bk. One, Ch.1 and Bk. Two, Ch.10). The fantasy is generally related in a plain style, with the narrator as witness more than participant, but perhaps the most compelling writing achieves its effect because it departs, dramatically, from balanced, emotional detachment and acquires an impressionistic fervour. Contrast the description of a Martian (p.132) with the instinctive revulsion at 'the strange horror of their appearance' (p.24), and the precise observation of the Handling Machines (p.131) with the terrified reaction to the tripod (p.50).

The realistic qualities of Wells's style are readily identifiable. The story repeatedly places the reader in familiar Home

Counties towns and villages, and the narrator walks through a Martian 'world' from Byfleet to Hyde Park, constantly identifying the debris of civilization. Suburban England at the turn of the century is continuously evoked, even as it is imaginatively destroyed. Excursionists, steam trains, gas lamps, 'Sunday raiment' and 'old-fashioned tricycles' are created in such profusion that the reader tends not to question Wells's disposal of them. The reportage of the account of the battle at Weybridge and Shepperton (Bk. One, Ch.12) and the exodus from the city (Bk. One, Ch.16) is superimposed upon an authentic portrayal of late 19th-century London. The first-hand impressions of war and flight are extraordinarily vivid, the style acquiring authority by its steady cataloguing of the 'horrible struggle' (see p.67 'The fighting was beginning.' and p.104 'They began to meet more people.').

In the early chapters particularly, Wells allows his sense of humour to give the style an almost satirical tone, through the accumulation of social observation, caricature, and idiosyncratic dialogue. A milkman declares that 'They aren't to be killed' if it can be helped, a 'potman' attempts to lock a 'lunatic' in the tap-room, boys throw stones at the cylinder, 'loafers' and ladies assemble in the expectation of seeing 'a heap of charred corpses'. And in the artilleryman's monologue we are told 'Cities, nations, civilization, progress – it's all over. That game's up. We're beat.'

Imagery in *The War of the Worlds* gives the fantasy a peculiar strength. Stars fall from heaven, pillars of fire are seen at Chobham, and a sword of heat brings hellfire and ashes to a suburbia guilty only of self-importance. Flight is a 'liquefaction of the social body', as if society putrefies under the onslaught of bacterial Martians. Life in either 'world' is viewed as a grim interdependence, as carrion crows squabble over the remains of humans destroyed by Martians in a pit of blood-coloured light. The narrator resurrects himself from the dead only to find a cadaverous city, shrouded in black. As the novel reaches its climax, the rhythm of the prose quickens and the style affects Biblical cadences (Bk. Two, Ch.9, pp.179–80). Nature triumphs over the universal schemer; intelligence must submit to what is biologically inevitable: 'For neither do men live or die in vain'. It is ironic that this rejector of any metaphysical interpretation of the universe in favour of a purely materialistic one should express the idea in the impressive prose of a religious inheritance. Finally, images of nightmare dominate as 'mad distortions of humanity' haunt the narrator. This impressionism (p.192) is what gives to the style it myth-creating quality.

General questions

1 Show how the novel, fantastic as it is, plays upon fairly ordinary fears.

Suggested note form answer

Individuals may fear what is possible, if not necessarily probable:
war, invasion, colonization
catastrophe, man-made or natural
hunger and privation
separation from and loss of loved ones
the breakdown of social order
the rapid collapse of a complex, interdependent society
loss of the familiar
being weak, persecuted, hunted
being alone
what Time, the future may bring

Develop several of these ideas, illustrating each by referring closely to the story and by quoting from it.
NB Before attempting to answer the questions below note carefully

a the timing and location of the arrival of each cylinder
b the strategic responses of the authorities to the invasion
c information given on the reasons for the invasion
d all details given of the Martians
e all information given on Martian technology.

2 Is *The War of the Worlds* a scientific fairy tale?

3 How important to the story are personal relationships?

4 What differing responses to the invasion do the principal characters illustrate?

5 How does H. G. Wells give a documentary realism to the novel?

6 Which scenes are most vivid and why?

7 'The most interesting parts of the story are the reflections of the narrator.' How far do you agree with this statement?

8 How does H. G. Wells create the impression of a self-approving, developing civilization at the turn of the century?

9 How may the invaders be likened to humans?

10 Do you agree that the chief effect of the novel is its 'dethronement' of Man?

11 What view of Nature is presented in the novel?

12 Give an account of the course of the war.

13 How far do you agree with the view that the ending of the novel is reassuring?

Further reading

The Time Machine H. G. Wells (Pan)
Selected Short Stories H. G. Wells (Penguin)
The Early H. G. Wells B. Bergonzi (Manchester University Press)
The Time Traveller: The Life of H. G. Wells Norman and Jeanne Mackenzie (Weidenfield and Nicolson)
H. G. Wells in *Writers and Critics* series P. Parrinder (Oliver and Boyd)

Pan study aids Titles published in the Brodie's Notes series

W. H. Auden Selected Poetry

Jane Austen Emma Mansfield Park Northanger Abbey Persuasion
Pride and Prejudice

Anthologies of Poetry Ten Twentieth Century Poets The Poet's Tale
The Metaphysical Poets

Samuel Beckett Waiting for Godot

Arnold Bennett The Old Wives' Tale

William Blake Songs of Innocence and Experience

Robert Bolt A Man for All Seasons

Harold Brighouse Hobson's Choice

Charlotte Brontë Jane Eyre

Emily Brontë Wuthering Heights

Robert Browning Selected Poetry

John Bunyan The Pilgrim's Progress

Geoffrey Chaucer (parallel texts editions) The Franklin's Tale
The Knight's Tale The Miller's Tale The Nun's Priest's Tale
The Pardoner's Tale Prologue to the Canterbury Tales
The Wife of Bath's Tale

Richard Church Over the Bridge

John Clare Selected Poetry and Prose

Samuel Taylor Coleridge Selected Poetry and Prose

Wilkie Collins The Woman in White

William Congreve The Way of the World

Joseph Conrad The Nigger of the Narcissus & Youth
The Secret Agent

Charles Dickens Bleak House David Copperfield Dombey and Son
Great Expectations Hard Times Little Dorrit Oliver Twist
Our Mutual Friend A Tale of Two Cities

Gerald Durrell My Family and Other Animals

George Eliot Middlemarch The Mill on the Floss Silas Marner

T. S. Eliot Murder in the Cathedral Selected Poems

J. G. Farrell The Siege of Krishnapur

Henry Fielding Joseph Andrews

F. Scott Fitzgerald The Great Gatsby

E. M. Forster Howards End A Passage to India
Where Angels Fear to Tread

William Golding Lord of the Flies The Spire

Oliver Goldsmith Two Plays of Goldsmith: She Stoops to Conquer;
The Good Natured Man

Graham Greene Brighton Rock The Power and the Glory
The Quiet American

Thom Gunn and Ted Hughes Selected Poems

Thomas Hardy Chosen Poems of Thomas Hardy
Far from the Madding Crowd Jude the Obscure
The Mayor of Casterbridge Return of the Native
Tess of the d'Urbervilles The Trumpet-Major

L. P. Hartley The Go-Between The Shrimp and the Anemone

Joseph Heller Catch-22

Ernest Hemingway For Whom the Bell Tolls
The Old Man and the Sea

Barry Hines A Kestrel for a Knave

Gerard Manley Hopkins Poetry and Prose of Gerard Manley Hopkins

Aldous Huxley Brave New World

Henry James Washington Square

Ben Jonson The Alchemist Volpone

James Joyce A Portrait of the Artist as a Young Man

John Keats Selected Poems and Letters of John Keats

Ken Kesey One Flew over the Cuckoo's Nest

Rudyard Kipling Kim

D. H. Lawrence The Rainbow Selected Tales Sons and Lovers

Harper Lee To Kill a Mockingbird

Laurie Lee As I Walked out One Midsummer Morning
Cider with Rosie

Thomas Mann Death in Venice & Tonio Kröger

Christopher Marlowe Doctor Faustus Edward the Second

W. Somerset Maugham Of Human Bondage

Gavin Maxwell Ring of Bright Water

Arthur Miller The Crucible Death of a Salesman

John Milton A Choice of Milton's Verse Comus and Samson Agonistes Paradise Lost I, II

Sean O'Casey Juno and the Paycock
The Shadow of a Gunman and the Plough and the Stars

George Orwell Animal Farm 1984

John Osborne Luther

Alexander Pope Selected Poetry

J. B. Priestley An Inspector Calls

Siegfried Sassoon Memoirs of a Fox-Hunting Man

Peter Shaffer The Royal Hunt of the Sun

William Shakespeare Antony and Cleopatra As You Like It Coriolanus Hamlet Henry IV (Part I) Henry IV (Part II) Henry V Julius Caesar King Lear Love's Labour's Lost Macbeth Measure for Measure The Merchant of Venice A Midsummer Night's Dream Much Ado about Nothing Othello Richard II Richard III Romeo and Juliet The Sonnets The Taming of the Shrew The Tempest Twelfth Night The Winter's Tale

G. B. Shaw Androcles and the Lion Arms and the Man
Caesar and Cleopatra The Doctor's Dilemma Pygmalion Saint Joan

Richard Sheridan Plays of Sheridan: The Rivals; The Critic;
The School for Scandal

John Steinbeck The Grapes of Wrath Of Mice and Men & The Pearl

Tom Stoppard Rosencrantz and Guildenstern are Dead

J. M. Synge The Playboy of the Western World

Jonathan Swift Gulliver's Travels

Alfred Tennyson Selected Poetry

William Thackeray Vanity Fair

Flora Thompson Lark Rise to Candleford

Dylan Thomas Under Milk Wood

Anthony Trollope Barchester Towers

Mark Twain Huckleberry Finn

Keith Waterhouse Billy Liar
Evelyn Waugh Decline and Fall Scoop
H. G. Wells The History of Mr Polly The War of the Worlds
John Webster The White Devil
Oscar Wilde The Importance of Being Earnest
Virginia Woolf To the Lighthouse
William Wordsworth The Prelude (Books 1, 2)
John Wyndham The Chrysalids
W. B. Yeats Selected Poetry